EXPLORING HISTORY
The Vikings

SYDNEY WOOD

Oliver & Boyd

Oliver & Boyd
Robert Stevenson House
1–3 Baxter's Place
Leith Walk
Edinburgh EH1 3BB

A Division of Longman Group UK Ltd

First published 1977
Sixth impression 1988

Selections and editorial matter
© Sydney Wood 1977. All rights reserved; no part of this publication may be reproduced, stored in a retrieval system, or transmitted in any form or by any means, electronic, mechanical, photocopying, recording, or otherwise without either the prior written permission of the Publishers or a licence permitting restricted copying in the United Kingdom issued by the Copyright Licensing Agency Ltd, 33-34 Alfred Place, London, WC1E 7DP.

ISBN 0 05 003047 7

Produced by Longman Group (FE) Ltd
Printed in Hong Kong

Contents

1. A mysterious people 3
2. The Vikings at home 6
3. The Vikings at work 17
4. Viking beliefs 22
5. Viking ships 26
6. Viking warriors 32
7. The Vikings in Britain 39
Bibliography 48

Topics for Workguides

1. A mysterious people
2. The Vikings at home
3. The Vikings at work
4. Viking beliefs
5. Viking ships
6. Viking warriors
7. The Vikings in Britain

ACKNOWLEDGEMENTS

The author and publishers wish to thank the following for permission to reproduce photographs on the undernoted pages:
Arnamagean Institute (photo: Arne Mann Nielsen) 14 (upper); Biblioteca Nacional, Madrid 38; Anne Bolt 6; Controller of Her Majesty's Stationary Office (Crown copyright) 39 (upper); Department of the Environment (Crown copyright) 41, 42; Alan King 43; National Museum, Copenhagen, Denmark, 24, 25 (left), 35; National Museum of Antiquities of Scotland 14 (lower), 34, 39 (right); National Museum of Iceland 8, 23 (upper); National Museum of Ireland 7; Phaidon Press 11 (lower), 13, 17 (bottom left), 27, 47; Schleswig-Holsteinisches Landesmuseum für Vor- und Frühgesichte 20; State Historical Museum, Stockholm, Sweden 12 (right), 16 (right), 18 (lower), 19 (centre bottom), 21, 22, 23 (lower), 28 (lower); University Museum of National Antiquities, Oslo, Norway (copyright), 2, 9, 10, 11 (upper), 12 (top left), 16 (left), 17 (3 items—right), 18 (upper), 18–19 (centre bottom), 19 (top and right), 26, 28 (upper), 29, 32, 33; York Archaeological Trust 4, 12 (bottom left), 44, 45; Yorkshire Museum 25 (right).

A Viking burial mound site in Norway.

1 A mysterious people

The Mound

Imagine you are spending your summer holidays abroad, staying at a lonely farmhouse. On your first morning you go exploring and, upon climbing to the top of a hill, you look down and see the sort of thing shown in the picture on the opposite page.

1. Do you think this mound looks as if it is man-made?
2. What sort of reasons can you suggest for your answer?
3. Look carefully at the shape of the mound and see if you can offer any suggestions as to why it was made, and what sort of things might be found inside it or under it.

The Dig

You decide to explore your discovery.

1. In order to investigate the mysterious mound more fully, what sort of tools would you need?
2. Do you think it would be safe to dig anywhere?
3. Can you suggest a sensible plan about where to start digging?

Certainly you will need expert help, so let us imagine you have been able to call upon an archaeologist to come and assist you. Here is a picture of archaeologists at work.

1. Study the picture and make a list of the kinds of tools and instruments being used.
2. In a short sentence explain what each one is for. During your dig you will have to work very carefully for, if you find anything, it might be very old and fragile or, perhaps, made of a delicate material.
3. Explain the kind of work done by an archaeologist.

Probably the archaeologist will suggest that you measure the site, draw a plan of it, then dig into it in one section.

You will have to mark on the section where anything you find was placed.

1. If some things are found much more deeply buried than others, what might this mean?

Archaeologists at work.

Investigating a section of a burial mound.

![Find from excavation of Viking site at York ('dress fastener').](find)

Find from excavation of Viking site at York ('dress fastener').

The Finds

After days of exhausting work, the trowel you are using uncovers an object like the one on the left.

1. *What do you think it is?*
2. *Does it seem to be for decoration or practical use? (Since it has a pin on the back it might possibly have been used to support some kind of clothing.)*

With growing excitement you uncover more and more objects until you are able to lay quite a number on the ground. This is what they look like:

Since an archaeologist needs to record his finds carefully, you could set out your list of finds like this:

Date of find	Drawing of find	Place where object found	Sentences describing it and what it might be
1. 2. 3. etc.			

Let us examine the objects you have found. Some are easy to label – bowls, jewellery, money – but

1. *What are the objects labelled 5?*
2. *Which of the objects you have found are likely to be very helpful in finding out how old these things are?*

The archaeologist will have to help you with items 5, for these are items connected with weaving. The Vikings used upright looms propped against a wall, and they started weaving from the top and worked downwards.

Coins nowadays have dates on them and, though this was not always so, they often have a name or sign to show who the important person was who ordered them to be made. Since coins might have been used for many many years, however, this just gives a very rough date. *Carbon dating*, the scientific study of animal and vegetable remains, also only gives a general guide about the age of objects found in an archaeological dig. Still, the archaeologist is able to tell you that these items are about 1000 years old and were buried around a body laid to rest under a burial mound.

What Sort of People made the Mound?

Using the list of objects you have helped to find, try to work out what kind of people made and used these objects.

1. Do they seem to have been a peaceful or warlike folk?
2. Do you think they deserve to be called 'civilised'?

Look at the clever designs worked into the objects; notice that money is being used. It is quite likely that you would say to the archaeologist that the makers of the mound were peaceful farmers and craftsmen. Imagine how you might then feel if the archaeologist laughed and began to tell you about a book he had been reading concerning the people who made these objects. The book was written many centuries ago. The archaeologist tells you that in the year 793

a fierce raiding band of these people sailed to a peaceful abbey in England called Lindisfarne. There they killed many monks and took others prisoner. They seized precious things from the abbey, smashed the church and library, set fire to the buildings and killed all the sheep and cattle.

1. Now what do you think of your peaceful and civilised craftsmen-farmers?
2. Can you suggest other sorts of ways of clearing up the mystery?
3. The archaeologist has given you an account written a hundred years after 793 by the raiders' enemies (in a book called The Anglo-Saxon Chronicle)*. Does this mean you should believe it?*

This has been, so far, an imaginary investigation. Such burials do exist, especially in Scandinavia, for these people were the Vikings. There are several ways of finding out more about them.
(1) The Vikings left many other kinds of objects besides those already described.
(2) Friends and enemies wrote about them.
(3) They wrote and carved a little themselves.
(4) They told stories that were eventually written down.
(5) Some traces of places they built can be found.
(6) Some place names show where Vikings once lived.
(7) Some Vikings conquered the part of France known now as Normandy.
    A tapestry, called the Bayeux Tapestry, was made for these 'Northmen' and shows many details of Viking life.

2 The Vikings at home

The Viking Homelands

A north German, called Adam of Bremen, who lived at the time of the Vikings wrote about Scandinavia:

The soil in Jutland is sterile except for places close to a river, nearly everything looks like a desert. Norway is the most barren of all countries because of its rugged mountains and extreme cold. But part of Sweden is fertile, the land is rich in fruits and honey.

Troll Fjord, Norway.

The Viking Homelands.

1. Write down the names of the countries where the Vikings lived.
2. Trace the map above. Colour in green the areas where you think it would be easy to grow food. Write a sentence giving a reason for your answer.
3. Do you think that many Vikings would have lived far from the sea?
4. What do you think 'sterile' soil is like?

The picture on the left shows the kind of place where many Norwegian Vikings lived.

1. If you were coming to live here, along with other settlers, in what position would you build your homes?
2. Look carefully at the picture and try and work out how an early settler would earn his living in these surroundings.

Viking Houses

1. If you came to live in a place like the one in the photograph on page 6, and had only a few simple tools (of which an axe would be the most important), what would you make your house from?
2. Winters are very cold. You have no glass. How do you think you would plan a house to cope with these problems? Make a sketch of what your house might look like.
3. What would you use for building in areas with few or no trees?

In an area like the fjord in the photograph, where many trees grow, it would be sensible to build a wooden house near the shore, and this is just what Vikings usually did.

Archaeologists have dug up the sites of many buildings left by the Vikings. Over many years timber may rot away, but even when it does holes and marks are left in the ground in the places where posts once stood. From these it is possible to work out what one kind of Viking house might have looked like.

1. Copy the drawing on the right.
2. Write down next to the various parts of the house what they are made of. The walls, for instance, are made of halved tree trunks.
3. Can you suggest why the building has no windows and no chimney?
4. Some Viking homes had walls made of timber posts placed well apart. How do you think the spaces between the posts might have been filled?
5. Why were these buildings called 'longhouses'?

Viking house site excavation showing remains of post and wattle wall (Dublin).

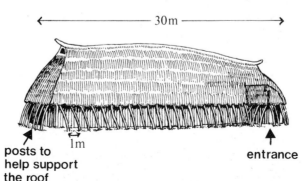

Trelleborg house reconstruction, Jutland (artist's drawing).

Reconstruction of farmhouse at Stong, Iceland (artist's drawing).

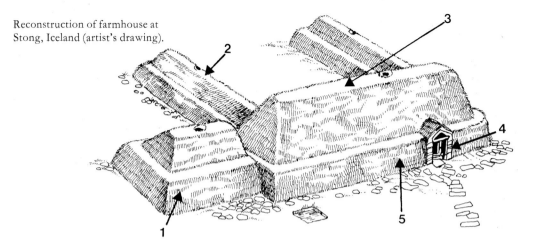

1. small hall
2. dairy (3 huge wooden vats stood in it to store dairy produce)
3. main hall (the original house) with central fireplace, benches lined the long side walls
   Small units for dairy, kitchen, storage, guest room added as need arose
4. entrance leads into small room screened from main hall
5. turf walls built up on 2 stone layers

This drawing shows another kind of Viking house built later than the Trelleborg house. Its walls were made of layers of turf and stone.

1. *In what ways is this house different from the Trelleborg house on page 7?*
2. *Why are its walls not made of timber?*

This beautifully written and decorated page comes from the Flateyjarbok, one of the great Sagas written in medieval Iceland.

We can also find out more about Viking life from documents like that shown at the foot of this page.

It is part of one of the sagas. Sagas were stories written by Viking settlers in Iceland, mostly in the twelfth and thirteenth centuries. They were recorded on specially scraped and softened calfskin called *vellum*. The writer used a quill pen and boiled berry juice. These stories were great adventure tales that Vikings had told for many years, but they were written down well after the Viking age. They are full of fanciful ideas but do give information about Viking life. In one a house is described:

Gunnar's sleeping hall was made entirely of wood and covered in wooden planks on the outside. There were window openings on either side of a ridgepole, with wooden shutters covering them.

Njal's Saga

1. *What sort of materials were Viking houses made from?*
2. *Viking houses changed as time passed. What is the chief difference between Gunnar's house and the houses in the pictures on pages 7 and 8?*
3. *Explain how archaeologists can work out what Viking homes were like, even when timber has rotted away.*
4. *Draw a plan of the Stong house (above). Say what the different rooms were used for? Which was the main living room?*

Inside a Viking House

One of the saga authors wrote

It was the custom that there should be large halls on the farms. Men would sit by the long fires in the evenings. It was there that tables were set in front of people and afterwards they would sleep beside the fires.

Grettir's Saga

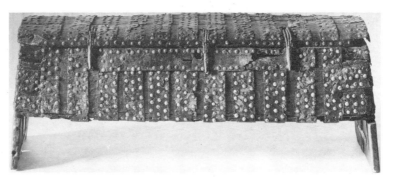

Chest and bed found when a Viking burial ship was excavated at Oseberg.
(There is a picture of a chair from the ship on page 16.)

Soapstone bowl.

1. How did Vikings light their houses?
2. What would bowls like the ones on this page be filled with to provide light?
3. What would be the danger in having a big fire in a house like the Trelleborg house?
4. How could the Vikings make a floor of earth less cold and uncomfortable?

Viking homes did not contain a lot of furniture. There were no cupboards. A number of articles of furniture were discovered when a Viking burial ship was excavated at Oseberg.

1. Where do you think Vikings would hang or store their clothes?
2. Describe in your own words what the furniture found in the Oseberg ship was like. You might like to illustrate some of the carvings.
3. The bed is very unusual. It was found with many other items that suggest it once belonged

Bowl on iron spike.

Models of a Viking jarl and his wife from a Norwegian Museum.

to a Viking Queen. Imagine you are the craftsman who made the bed and invent a story to explain how you won the order, searched for timber, made the bed and what the Queen said upon receiving it.

Different kinds of Vikings

A Viking poet described the different kinds of people in his country in a poem. The first group of people he dealt with were all like a man called Thrall.

> Rough were his hands
> With wrinkled skin
> With knuckles knotty
> With fingers thick
> His face was ugly
> His back was humpy.

Thrall's children had names like Lump, Noisy, Thicklegs and Lazybones.

Another group of people were like a young man called Earl.

> Blond his hair and bright his cheeks
> Eyes as fierce as a young serpent's
> Earl grew up in that same hall
> To shake a spear shaft, string a bow
> Ride on horseback, hunt with hounds
> Brandish swords, do feats of swimming.

Yet a third group of people did jobs like this

> Taming oxen, making plough frames,
> Raising house beams, building barns,
> Making carts and driving ploughs.

Rigspula (a Viking poem)

1. In Viking times there were three groups in society: slaves, freemen (or 'karls') and leaders (or 'jarls'). Which poem describes which of these groups?
2. What kind of jobs do you think the slaves did? Was it his work that probably made Thrall so ugly?
3. Look at the names of Thrall's children. What kinds of names do you think the children of the man in the second poem ought to have?

Vikings took their parents' names as their surnames. Thus Olaf, son of Erik, would be Olaf Eriksson. But they also loved giving people names according to their appearance or character, Magnus the Good or Harold Fairhair for example, or this lady

Hallgerd was beautiful and tall, that was why she was called Longlegs.

Njal's Saga

An Arab traveller, Ibn Fadlan, whose journeys brought him into contact with Vikings declared

Never before did I see men with more perfect bodies, tall as date palms with coppery fair hair.

Clothing and Appearance

1. Describe the kinds of clothes the people shown on these two pages are wearing.
2. What sort of material are they made from?

The saga writers described Viking clothes too.

Hallgerd wore a cloak of blue woven material and beneath it a scarlet skirt and silver belt about her waist.

Njal's Saga

Sybil wore a blue mantle fastened with straps and adorned with stones all the way down to the hem. She had a necklace of glass beads. On her head she wore a black lambskin hood lined with white cat's fur. On her feet she wore hairy calfskin shoes with long thick laces which had large tin buttons on the end. She wore catskin gloves with white fur inside.

Erik's Saga

He was wearing a blue tunic with a silver belt, blue striped trousers and black boots. His hair was combed well back and held in place with a silk band.

Njal's Saga

A Viking leader, King Magnus, marched into his last battle brandishing a sword he called 'Fishbone' and wearing a tunic that was half white and half red. When they could, Vikings bought silks from other lands.

Ibn Fadlan noticed

Every one of the women wears at her breast a metal box with a ring and knife attached of iron, silver, copper or gold according to her husband's wealth. They also wear neck rings of gold or silver.

These two tapestries show the sort of clothes Vikings wore. The top one is part of a tapestry found on the Oseberg ship and the bottom one part of the Bayeux Tapestry mentioned on page 5.

Jet and silver necklace from Norway.

Viking comb found at York.

Archaeologists have found many beautiful pieces of jewellery like the necklace here. Most other people of the times were not as clean as Vikings. A popular Viking poet declared

Guests should be greeted with water, a towel and a hearty welcome.

Há vamál (a Viking poem)

Bath houses have been found near many Viking homes, where they sat in the steam caused by pouring cold water on baking hot stones. An English writer said that the Danish Vikings who had settled in England combed their hair often, bathed every week and changed their linen underclothes frequently. Archaeologists have found many items like the comb on the left.

The Swedes seen by Ibn Fadlan, on the other hand, must have been unusual for he was horrified by them. 'They are as lousy as donkeys', he wrote.

1. Look carefully at the description of Sybil. Try and draw a picture of her or describe her in your own words.
2. What reasons can you list for suggesting that the Vikings were a clean people?
3. Do you think the clothes that they wore were suited to cold weather? Why?
4. From what you have read and looked at
   (a) do you think Vikings were fond of colours?
   (b) what makes you think they may have been fussy about their appearance?

Food

1. How do you think food might be cooked using objects like those shown below?
2. Since Vikings had to eat foods found nearby, what sort of animals might they catch?
3. What sorts of wild plants might also provide food?
4. How does Viking cooking differ from our cooking today?

Viking cooking utensils.

Viking farmers grew rye, barley and oats from which porridge or bread were made. The cattle, sheep and pigs they kept provided many good meals, and they ate horse flesh too. As well as milk, they drank mead made from honey, and beer.

Two meals a day were prepared, one in the early morning and the other in the evening. Every Viking had a knife for cutting food, but no forks were used. The food was served on plates, in bowls or on thick hunks of bread, and drinks were usually taken from animal horns. These are descriptions of different meals written by a Viking poet.

> Coarse bread brought to them
> Thick and heavy and full of *husks*
> [*outer skin of grain*]
> In the middle of the board
> In the bowl was broth.
>
> Then mother took a patterned cloth of fine linen
> Loaves of thin bread, light, made of wheat
> She then carried in
> Meat well browned and fully cooked birds
> There was wine in a bowl, bright were the goblets.
>
> *Rigspula*

1. Which of these two meals would you have preferred?
2. Explain how the two meals differ.
3. Can you think of any reason why they are different?

Adam of Bremen wrote of the Vikings

They consider it shameful to deny good cheer to a traveller and there is keen competition among them for the privilege of entertaining a stranger.

1. What does this tell you about Vikings' attitude to strangers?
2. Is this how you would treat a stranger today?
3. In the picture below, what items can you see that are like those in use today?

Cooking scene from the Bayeux Tapestry.

Leisure

The following items will tell you some of the ways Vikings spent their spare time.

Illustration from the *Jónsbók*, Iceland.

Part of the set of Viking chessmen discovered on the Island of Lewis, Scotland.

The seven year old Egil, beaten in a ball game by an older boy called Grim, was so furious that he went home for an axe and went up to the game where Grim had just got the ball and hit it away, the other boys running after it. Then Egil ran to Grim and swung the axe into his head so that it reached the brain.

Egil's Saga

The horses went at each other and bit each other for a long time without having to be goaded on.

Njal's Saga

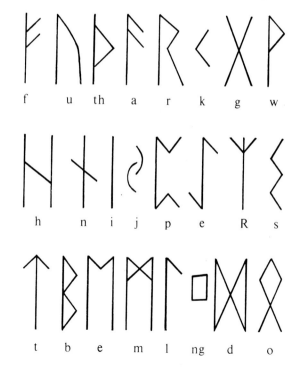

Runic alphabet (see also Rune stone on p. 19). Notice how the letters are made from easily cut straight lines.

1. Which, if any, of these games are played today?
2. From this evidence, do you think Vikings were kind and gentle people? Why?
3. What sort of a person do you think Egil was?
4. Are there any games played today that are violent? If so, which?
5. Why do you think Viking writing, which was carved on rock and wood, had so many straight lines in it?

Law and Order

A party of Vikings were travelling to a meeting called a Thing. Two of them, Grettir and Skeggi, began to quarrel about who owned a bag of food they had found. Skeggi seized his axe but Grettir grabbed the handle and smashed the axe into Skeggi's head, killing him. Their leader Thorkell, realised Skeggi was missing and that Grettir had killed him. They rode on to the Thing and there the matter was taken up by Skeggi's relatives. Thorkell agreed to pay them compensation. Grettir was banished for three years.

Grettir's Saga

1. From this saga extract, how were Vikings guilty of crimes punished?
2. How do you think Skeggi's family might have treated Grettir after the 'Thing's' decision?
3. Does this 'Thing' remind you of any kind of meeting of people today? If so, what?

According to the sagas, quarrels between families that began with an incident like this could go on for years. Vikings lived in small-sized settlements and it wasn't easy for a criminal to hide his crime. A number of other writings about Viking laws have survived.

If a man carries hot trough iron [*hot iron to be carried to a trough*] the trough is to be twelve paces away. When the iron has been thrown in the trough a mitten is placed over the hand. It shall be opened in three days.

Skane Law

This was to see if the hand was healing up.

1. What do you think a test like this was meant to prove?
2. Do you think it is a sensible way of deciding someone's guilt? Why?

There were all sorts of fines for crimes. Sometimes two Vikings settled their quarrel by fighting a duel.

The Importance of Women in Society

Thorberg was a person of great magnificence and tremendously wise. She was the leading personality in the district and managed everything when Vermund was away.

Grettir's Saga

There was a wealthy man called Thorvald. With his friend Osvif he set out to see Hoskuld. He asked if he might marry Hoskuld's daughter who was called Hallgerd. 'Name the conditions', Thorvald said. 'I will not let her quick temper stand in the way of this arrangement.' They discussed it. Hoskuld did not ask his daughter's opinion because he was eager to marry his daughter off. They agreed terms and thereupon Thorvald was bethrothed to Hallgerd. The wedding feast went well and Hoskuld paid Hallgerd's dowry.

Njal's Saga

1. When do you think Thorberg would have to manage everything for long periods?

2. What sort of a person was Hallgerd?
3. How does the way her marriage was arranged differ from the way marriages are arranged now?
4. What is a dowry?

Viking women had important jobs to do (see the next chapter), and though their marriages were arranged for them, it was possible to get a divorce. Probably the ideal Viking woman was someone like Bergthora, wife of Njal. She would not leave her husband's side to escape a blazing farmhouse saying

I was given young to Njal and I have promised him that one fate shall fall on both of us.

Njal's Saga

Chair found on the Oseberg ship (see p. 9).

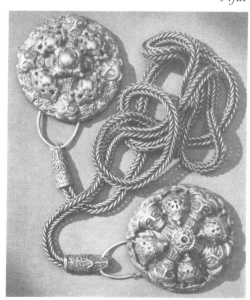

Viking jewellery from Sweden.

3 The Vikings at work

Farmers

These pictures and extracts will help you to see how Vikings obtained food.

A writer of Viking times noticed, in Norway,

> They browse their cattle far off in the solitudes [*lonely places*]. In this way do the people make a living from livestock by using the milk of the flocks and herds and the wool for clothing.
>
> Adam of Bremen

A saga author wrote about a Viking farmer

> When Skallagrim's stock had increased it was all sent up into the hills in the summer.
>
> Skallagrim had men rowing out for fish, catching seals and collecting eggs. There were often stranded whales and anyone could shoot them who wanted.
>
> *Egil's Saga*

1. What is the man on the left in the picture below doing?
2. What kind of animal is he using?

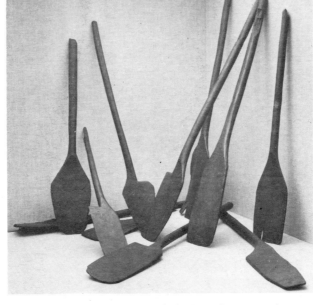

3. What do you think the machine he is working is probably made of?
4. What is the man in the middle of the picture doing? How is this work done today?
5. What are the spades made of? Would they be good tools to use?
6. What are the implements in the picture above right used for?
7. With tools like these, do you think Viking farmers lived a hard life? Give reasons.
8. Why do you think Skallagrim moved his animals up into the hills in summer?
9. What use would Vikings make of the seals and whales they had killed?

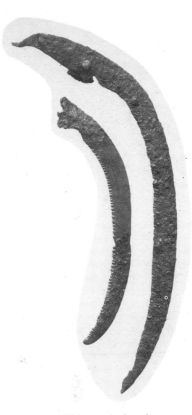

Viking agricultural implements: (above left) spades, (above) sickles, and (below) stone hand quern for grinding corn.

Farming scene from the border of the Bayeux Tapestry.

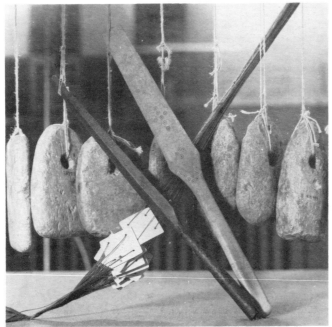

Items used by Vikings for weaving.

Craftsmen

1. Why would Vikings who were farmers have to be able to do all sorts of different jobs?

Most Viking homes contained objects like those in the picture on the left.

1. Try and work out what each was for.
2. Which members of the family do you think used these objects?
3. From what you have read so far, what kind of raw material do you think was used to make cloth?
4. Do you think it would have been easy to make clothes in Viking times? Give reasons.
5. Can you suggest how Vikings might colour their clothing?

While women made clothing, shaping wood and iron was man's work.

1. Draw or list the tools illustrated on the left and write next to each what you think it was used for.
2. What tools would a modern carpenter have that are missing from this Viking set?

Carpenter's tools found at Mastemyr, Gotland, Sweden.

1. Draw or list the tools illustrated on the right (top centre), and write next to each what you think it was used for.
2. How would the smith soften and shape his iron?

Most large farms had forges, but some Vikings spent their lives as craftsmen.

1. What kinds of things might it be difficult for ordinary farmers to make for themselves — the rest of the pictures on this page may help you here.

Blacksmith's tools found at Bygland, Norway.

Keys made by Vikings.

Rune stone from Sweden.

Viking scissors or shears from Norway.

The site of Hedeby near the German-Danish border, (above) the excavated site and (below) an aerial view of the area.

Traders

1. *How does the site shown here differ from the Viking building sites we have looked at so far?*
2. *Why might skilled craftsmen have come here?*

These are pictures of Hedeby, the largest of Viking towns. It lay in a part of Southern Denmark near a river mouth and close to the Baltic Sea. This area is now in West Germany.

1. *Why do you think Vikings chose to build a town in such a place?*
2. *What sort of people might live here, as well as craftsmen?*

To towns like Hedeby came Viking traders. Read the following extracts:

I sail north to get walruses, for they have a noble bone in their tusks and their hide is very good for ships' ropes.

Ottar, a Norwegian Viking

As soon as the Viking ships were moored the Vikings came on land. Each man carried bread, meat, onions, milk, and walked to a tall wooden post with a human face carved on it. The man casts himself down before the figure and says 'Oh Lord, I have come from afar with slave girls and furs'. He then lists his goods and says 'I beg you to bring me a rich buyer who will take all I have to sell'.

Ibn Fadlan

The Bishop noticed slaves for sale in Hedeby. One was a nun who was bowing and singing psalms. The Bishop offered her heathen captors valuables for her, but they insisted on having his horse. He therefore leapt from the saddle and gave them the horse. He gave the nun her freedom.

Life of Bishop Rimbert

Archaeologists have found in Viking lands objects like those illustrated here.

1. What sorts of things did Vikings trade in?
2. Where do you think they found their slaves?
3. What can you tell about Viking beliefs from the fact that they had a nun for sale as a slave?
4. Do you think the people who made the goods Vikings bought were more skilful than Viking craftsmen? Why?
5. What do the places these foreign objects came from show about Viking trade?

Hedeby was a town 28 hectares in size. It was burned to the ground in 1050 by an envious Norwegian Viking, Harald Hardrada. But archaeologists were still able to work out Hedeby's size because the rubbish piled up over the years had changed the colour of the soil.

The adventures of some traders are mentioned in sagas.

Then the merchant ship was attacked by a fleet of thirteen pirate Viking vessels. The pirates' leader shouted, 'We offer you two choices, either go ashore and let us seize your goods, or we will attack and kill every man we catch.' A fierce battle began and the merchants were only saved by the surprise arrival of ten vessels full of friendly Vikings. This time the merchants escaped. Their would-be robbers begged for mercy and it was granted them, but all their goods were taken from them.

Njal's Saga

1. What do you learn from this about the dangers faced by Viking traders?
2. Do you think the merchants were right to fight against such odds? Give reasons.
3. Do traders today face dangers like these?

Bronze flask, probably Persian, Eastern coins and jewellery from a Viking site.

4 Viking beliefs

Viking Burials

It was the year 921. Ibn Fadlan, the brave Arab traveller, was in Russia. There he came upon Vikings busy piling wood in a huge mound around one of their ships. He questioned one of the Vikings and found out that a great Viking chief had died. The chief was going to be given the sort of burial a really important person deserved. But he was not going to be buried alone. A Viking told Ibn Fadlan, 'When a chief dies his family says to his slave girls and servants, "Which of you will die with him?" Then one says, "I will." It is mostly the slave girls who do this.'

That explained why a specially dressed girl was being given so much attention – and also being guarded very carefully. For several days the Vikings feasted and drank. Around their chief they laid his weapons and his precious possessions. They killed a dog, two horses, two oxen and a cock and a hen and put these by the body. Finally the chosen slave girl was killed too, and laid beside her master. A Viking set fire to the ship in which the bodies lay. In less than an hour the ship, the slave and the dead man were burned to ashes. The Vikings built a mound where the ship had stood.

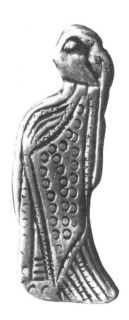

Two of the Valkyries.

In Scandinavia a different kind of burial was seen by another Arab traveller, Ibn Rustah.

When a great man among them dies, they make a grave like a large house and place him in it. With him they lay his clothes, the gold arm rings he wore, and also much food and drink and coins. They also lay his favourite wife in the grave with him while she is still alive. Then the door of the grave is blocked up and she dies there.

Vikings who were not very important were buried under mounds or memorial stones.
1. What kind of Viking was given a funeral with a burning ship?
2. What kind of objects were placed in the ship with the body?
3. Can you think of any reasons why Vikings should have their possessions buried with them?
4. What does the burying of the slave girl and the wife tell us about Viking views about women?
5. Do you think these Vikings were Christians? Give reasons for your opinion.

Gods

Vikings believed that there were many gods living in a place called 'Asgard'. They thought that Asgard was linked to our world, which they called 'Midgard', by a rainbow bridge. Beyond Asgard and Midgard lay Utgard, a stony wasteland inhabited by a race of giants who were the enemies of the gods.

An enormous snake lay around the world men lived in. It was called the Midgard serpent.

The greatest of the gods was Odin. He was the god of battles and of the dead, and also the god of poets and the wise. The eight-legged horse he rode was called Sleipnir. Two wolves, Geri and Freki, trotted alongside him. On his shoulders crouched two ravens, Hugin and Mugin, who told him all that was happening in the world. Although the Vikings believed Odin to be a great god, they did not trust him. He was gloomy because he knew all that would happen in the future; he was restless, travelled about constantly and was able to change himself into different kinds of creatures.

The figures on page 22 and bottom right on this page are Valkyries, carved figures of the female servants who visited the battlefields of men for Odin, choosing great warriors whom they took to the hall of Valhalla in Asgard. There the dead heroes feasted on boar and mead, hunted and fought, while waiting to follow Odin to a great last battle with the giants.

Thor is illustrated top right. Many Vikings were named after him with names like Thorkell and Thorstein. Thor cared for ordinary folk, especially farmers and fishers. He was honest, cheerful and generous, though he had a fierce temper and in a rage might well hurl the hammer you can see him holding. This magical hammer, after striking its target, flew back into Thor's hands. His chariot, as it crashed through the sky pulled by goats, made the sound men knew as thunder.

There were many other gods. One of them, called Loki, was cunning and dangerous and hated his fellow gods. Loki's children were monsters – and included the Midgard Serpent, a giant wolf and the Goddess Hel who ruled over the underworld where dead Vikings went who had failed to die nobly. Loki brought punishment upon himself by causing the death of the most generous, gentle, peaceful and intelligent of the gods, Balder. The whole of nature – rocks, fire, animals, plants, diseases – had sworn not to harm Balder. But the gods had forgotten to make mistletoe take the promise and from mistletoe Loki made an arrow. He tricked the blind god Hodr into firing it and killing Balder.

Then there was Frey. As a saga writer put it

Frey is beautiful in looks and mighty. He rules the rain and the sunshine and has power over all that grows in the ground. It is well to make vows to him for good seasons and peace.

Ynglinga Saga

Viking gods were full of faults. They quarrelled and cheated, as well as behaving nobly. Their watchman, Heimdall, could even hear grass

Thor holding his hammer. This is the actual size of the statue which is made of bronze.

One of the Valkyries.

Thor hammer charm.

growing in the ground or wool growing on sheep. But he could not stop the great battle between gods and giants called 'Ragnarok'.

On this terrible day, a day full of fire and thunder, Odin will be swallowed by the monster wolf, Thor and the Midgard serpent will kill each other, and the whole of Midgard, Asgard and Utgard will be destroyed. Yet from it a finer, purer place will emerge. Balder and Hodr will return to lead a better race of gods, and a finer race of men will appear too.

Asgard's Saga

In sagas and poems the Vikings wrote what they believed about the fierce gods who ruled men's lives.

1. Which of the gods do you think was preferred by
   (a) Viking leaders?
   (b) ordinary Vikings?
2. What do you think about the kind of heaven that Vikings believed in?

If plague or famine threaten, they offer a gift to Thor; if war to Odin; if marriage is to be celebrated – to Frey.

Adam of Bremen

1. How is Viking worship (described here) different from Christian worship? Does Viking worship seem in any way similar to worship in any religions today?

Vikings lived in a world full of dangers and mysteries, and gods helped to explain them. The dead, they thought, could come out of their graves and either help men or do great harm to them. There were elves and dwarves. Meadows, woods and springs all had their magic spirits. Other things were magical too.

Egil met a friend whose daughter was sick. A neighbour had carved runes and placed them under the girl's pillow to try and cure her. Egil read the runes, scraped them off and burned the whalebone and said, 'I counted ten crude runes cut on that piece of bone. They've done great harm to your daughter's health.' Egil then carved runes and placed them under the pillow where she lay. It seemed to her as though she woke from sleep and then she said that she was well.

Egil's Saga

1. What does this tell you about how Vikings regarded runes?
2. In honour of which god do you think Vikings might wear the charm illustrated on this page?
3. Why do you think Vikings might have worn charms?

They have their wizards who have power over Vikings' goods as if they were their own. The wizards order the Vikings to make offerings of women, men and cattle, just as they choose. The wizard takes the human or animal away, ties a rope about its neck and hangs it from a pole till it dies, saying 'This is an offering to the Gods'.

Ibn Rustah

1. Can you suggest another word for 'wizards'.
2. Why do you think the Vikings allowed them so much power?

In Sweden at Uppsala there is a temple entirely covered in gold. In it the people worship the statues of three gods. Thor occupies a throne in the middle, Odin and Frey have places on either side. Every nine years there is a feast for people from all over Sweden. People send gifts to Uppsala. They sacrifice nine of every living thing that is made and hang the bodies from a sacred tree near the temple.

Adam of Bremen

1. From looking at and reading this evidence, what do you think of Viking worship?
2. From what you have read so far, what number do you think the Vikings probably thought was magical?
3. At what sort of times did Vikings worship Thor, Odin and Frey?
5. How do you think Viking gods regarded people who were weak, or sick, or feeble from old age?

Christianity

It took a long time to win the Vikings from their old religion to Christianity. Many missionaries travelled to the Viking lands and tried, especially, to win over Viking leaders. Once a king or chief changed to Christianity he was likely to make ordinary people nearby follow him.

Helgi the Lean believed in Christ, yet he made vows to Thor for sea journeys or in tight corners and for everything he thought very important.

1. From the evidence on this page, how can we tell that for many years Vikings believed in Christianity and their old gods at the same time?

(You can find out more about Viking religion, if you wish, in *The Vikings*, a book in the *Then and There* series.)

This mould which belonged to a Jutland trader showed how he could cast both Christian crosses and the Thor hammer charm.

The Middleton Cross from Middleton, Yorkshire.

5 Viking ships

The Gokstad Ship

1. What is the object these men are uncovering?
2. Can you think of any reasons why it was buried so far from the sea?

Below left is the carefully restored ship that was excavated.

1. Do you think this ship needed deep water to sail in?
2. What sorts of power moved the ship along?
3. What kind of wood do you think Vikings preferred to use for such fine vessels?
4. Look back at the Craftsmen section of Chapter 2. What kinds of tools would Vikings need to make this ship?
5. How do you think the Vikings would have stopped water leaking between planking?
6. How is the ship steered? Is this how ships today are steered?

The Gokstad ship was made of oak. The overlapping planking (a style called *clinker built*) had a mixture of tar and rope or woollen cloth to plug gaps between planks. The ship could sail in water which was little more than a metre deep.

Uncovering the Gokstad ship in 1880.

Model of the Gokstad ship.

1. What tools are these boat builders using?
2. Why would it be useful to have a ship able to sail in shallow water?

Different Sorts of Ship

Thorolf had his ship made ready and loaded it with dried fish, cloth and skins of all sorts. On top of these he added furs. They went to England and loaded there with wheat and honey, wine and cloth. It had much paint work above the water line and a sail coloured in blue and red stripes.

Egil's Saga

1. Do you think the Gokstad ship would have been suitable transport for such a cargo?
2. Write down the differences between the Gokstad ship and that shown in the diagram here.
3. The diagram shows a knarr, used for trading and exploring. What is it that makes it more suitable for this work than a longship like the Gokstad ship?

Shipbuilding scene from the Bayeux Tapestry.

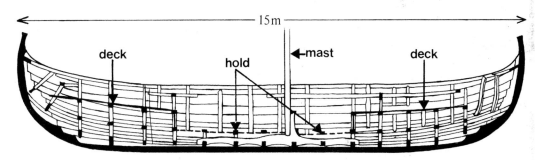

Diagram of a knarr.

Ships under sail from the Bayeux Tapestry.

Figurehead from the Oseberg ship.

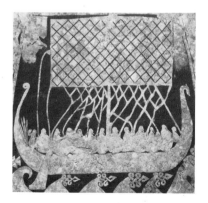

Carving of a ship from the Gotland Stone.

4. Do you think it would be easy to row a knarr?
5. Look back through chapter 3 and see if you can suggest what kinds of goods a knarr might have carried.
6. Do you think Thorolf was proud of his ship? Why?
7. Ships that have been found no longer have their sails. How do you think we might find out more about sails?

Saga writers describe sail patterning as striped but this carving (bottom left) shows a different design. Perhaps it is a rope net to strengthen the sail.

1. Yachts today don't usually have sails like these. Can you suggest any difficulties that might face Vikings in ships powered by single sails like those in the pictures?
2. Why do you think ships were so important to Vikings? It will help you to answer this if you look at the map at the beginning of Chapter 2.

Viking ships did many different jobs in war and peace. Their owners often gave them names, like *Strider* (the name of a fast ship) and *Sea Raven*. Not only were the ships painted, they were decorated with carvings too.

1. Look at the figureheads on the ships (pages 27 and 28). What kind of creatures are shown?
2. Do you think these creatures look fierce? Can you suggest why Vikings fitted such figureheads?

Travelling on a Viking Ship

If you had been going on a journey on a Viking ship you would need to take all sorts of things with you.

1. List and name the objects illustrated on the next page.
2. What kinds of foods do you think Vikings stored in the barrels? Remember the food might have to last many days.
3. Do you think the Vikings used the cooking pot for heating food while on board ship?
4. Vikings did not have modern means of navigation, so how do you think they found their way by sea?

This quotation is from an 1130 *Book of Settlements*

From Hernan in Norway you are to keep sailing west for Hvarf in Greenland, and then you will sail north of Shetland so that you can first sight it in very clear weather, but south of the Faroes so that the sea appears half way up the mountain slopes, but to the south of Iceland so that you may sight birds and whales from it.

Landnamabok

1. What does this tell you about how Vikings managed to navigate by sea?

Across Seas and Rivers

1. Write down a list of goods in which Vikings traded with other lands.
2. Vikings from Sweden often explored different routes from those used by Vikings from Norway and Denmark. Look at where these countries are placed on the map and suggest which way their Viking peoples might have travelled.
3. What countries would Vikings reach if they sailed west across the Atlantic?
4. What dangers might they face on long voyages on the North Atlantic?
5. What kind of evidence will tell us that Vikings visited other lands?
6. Swedish Vikings travelled, traded and conquered as far as Constantinople. They were generally known as the Rus. Can you think which country they gave their name to?

The articles in the pictures on this page were part of the equipment carried aboard Viking ships.

Iceland had been known about in Europe before Viking times. An Irish monk, Dicuil, writing in 825 said

It is now thirty years since priests who lived on that island told me that in the summer the setting sun hides itself so little that whatever task a man wishes to perform, even to picking lice from his shirt, he can manage it as if in broad daylight.
Liber Mensura Orbis Terrae

1. Name an occupation followed by some of the people who lived in Iceland before the Vikings arrived there?
2. Would they be difficult people for Vikings to defeat?

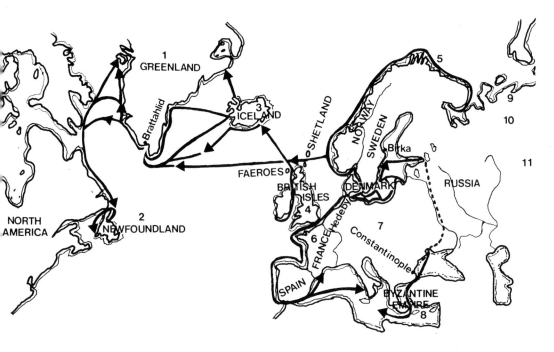

1. walrus ivory, furs, hides, woollens
2. timber, furs
3. fish, furs, woollens
4. wheat, woollens, tin, honey
5. walrus ivory, fish, hides
6. salt, wine
7. wine, slaves, pottery, glass, weapons, cloth, jewellery
8. silk, fruit, wine, jewellery, silver, spices
9. furs
10. slaves
11. slaves, furs, wax, honey, silver

The extent of Viking trade.

The Viking settlement of Iceland is reckoned to have taken place around the year 874. The first settlers were led by Ingolf Arnarson and built homes in a place called 'steamy bay' or Reykjavik. The Viking settlement there prospered. The settling of Greenland came later and is described in sagas:

Erik the Red and his men were sentenced as outlaws for killing other men. Erik said he was going to search for the land Gunnbjorn had glimpsed, and put to sea. He sailed south, explored to the west, went north in his third summer. Then he sailed back to Iceland. That summer he set off to colonise the country he had discovered, he named it Greenland for he said people would be tempted to go there if it had an attractive name.

Erik's Saga

1. Why do you think Erik was called 'the Red'?
2. Do you think Erik gave Greenland an accurate name? Give reasons for your answer.
3. Give reasons why you think Viking life in Greenland might have been more of a struggle than in Iceland.

A Viking community did grow up at Brattahlid.

The Vikings and North America

Bjarni Herjolfsson was a keen traveller abroad. On a journey to Greenland, winds and fogs overtook Bjarni and his men so that they had no idea where they were going. They sighted land and discussed where it might be. Bjarni said it could not be Greenland. They sailed in close and could see the country was not mountainous but was well wooded and with low hills. They sailed for two more days and sighted another land. Bjarni said it was no more Greenland than the first place. They sailed for more days and saw a third and then a fourth land 'This is very like what I am told about Greenland,' said Bjarni. 'Here we will land.' Bjarni gave an account of his travels.

There was much talk of voyages of discovery. Leif, son of Erik the Red, bought Bjarni's boat and found a crew of thirty-five. They sailed and found a flat country with forest. 'This land shall be called Markland,' said Leif. They sailed for two days to a land with an island off it. There was dew on the grass, to the men it seemed the sweetest thing they had tasted. There was no lack of salmon in the river. The country seemed so kind no winter fodder would be needed for livestock.

The Greenland Saga

1. Why would exploring be very dangerous work for Viking sailors?
2. The Vikings called the last-described land Vinland. Why do you think it was given this name?
3. Do you think Bjarni was right not to land in these strange lands? Why?
4. Descriptions in several sagas suggest that these lands which the Vikings reached were probably North America. What other evidence would help to prove this and show just where they settled?

Archaeologists have found in Newfoundland the remains of buildings that were lived in by Viking peoples. They have also found a Red Indian arrow head in Greenland.

1. What does the arrow head find suggest?
2. Would you think Vinland is likely to be Newfoundland? Give reasons.

Sea Fights

Vikings were as ready to fight on sea as on land. In one such action King Olaf of Norway's fleet sailed out to meet a huge force sent by the Kings of Denmark and Sweden and a Norwegian Earl. King Olaf's ships crashed into the enemy formation. Men hurled spears at one another and, when possible, boarded one another's vessels and fought with swords and axes. King Olaf was finally trapped on his famous ship, *Long Serpent*, and the saga writer, Snorri Sturluson, records

All the defenders went aft to join their king but strong and bold though they were, most fell. Rather than be taken Olaf leapt overboard in full armour, flung his shield over his head, and drowned.

Olaf Tryggvason's Saga

This was the kind of noble way a Viking was supposed to die.

6 Viking warriors

Viking helmet and mailcoat.

A Fight on Ice

One morning a Viking called Njal was awakened by a loud knocking on his door. He opened it to see his two sons, his son-in-law and two friends. At their head was Skarphedin with a small round shield and an axe. Next came Kari in a silken jacket and gilded helmet with a shield that had painted on it the figure of a lion. Helgi was in a helmet with a shield. All wore dyed clothes. After greeting Njal these five set off in search of an enemy called Thrain. They found him, but he was on the other side of an icy river and had seven men with him. They charged down to the river's edge. Thrain and his men stood on an icy patch near an ice floe. Skarphedin, with axe raised ran down to the river. It was so deep there was no place to wade across. Skarphedin took a running start and leapt forward on to the icefloe with the speed of a bird. Thrain was just about to put on his helmet as Skarphedin bore down on him and struck him with his axe 'Battle Troll'. The axe split Thrain's head right down so that his teeth dropped on to the ice. This happened so quickly that no one could strike at Skarphedin and he continued to glide along the ice at great speed.

'Now that's fighting like a real man,' said Kari. Tjorvi hurled his spear at Kari, but Kari leaped up and the spear flew harmlessly beneath his feet. Kari dealt Tjorvi a sword blow that killed him.

Njal's Saga

Once three of their enemies were dead, Njal's sons let the rest go.

The sagas are full of fierce fights like this. An Arab traveller, Ibn Miskawaih, wrote

Vikings do not know the meaning of the word defeat. They never turn their backs on their enemies but kill or are killed. A Viking fights with spear and shield. He wears a dagger and has a throwing spear.

1. What does the first story tell you about the kind of men that Vikings admired?
2. Write down in a list all the different weapons described here.
3. What kinds of things did these Vikings have with which to defend themselves?
4. What name did Skarphedin give to his battle axe?
5. How did Kari escape being wounded by a spear?

Viking Weapons

Archaeologists have found many weapons like those used in this fight.

1. How do you think a Viking would have fought with such a large, broad, two-edged sword as the one on the left of the picture below?
2. Why do you think there was a groove down the middle? It might help you to know Vikings called this the 'blood channel'.

Because they were so long, swords were quite difficult to make. The Vikings probably bought their finest swords from other lands, but they did make many themselves. Smiths melted and twisted thin iron bars together, by a method called 'pattern welding'. The sword was fitted with steel cutting edges and ground [worn down] and filed over and over again. Archaeologists trying to make a sword in the way Vikings did have found it takes nearly a month to produce one, properly fitted with its guard and handle.

Vikings loved their swords and thought they had special magical powers. They told stories of swords made by dwarves or given by Odin. They decorated the handles skilfully and gave swords names like 'Leg biter' or 'Gleam of Battle'. King Hakon had a sword called 'Quern biter' because it had split a stone quern in two.

1. Do you think all Viking men would have owned swords?

Tips of spears and arrows have survived in large numbers. Some spears were for throwing but others were large and heavy.

1. What would a spear too heavy for throwing have been used for?
2. How would it be best for men faced by all these weapons to try and defend themselves?
3. How would the items on page 32 protect you from attack?
4. What is the shield on this page made of? Would this make it unsatisfactory or can you think of any advantages in having a small light shield?
5. Why do you think the shield has a knob in the middle?
6. Do you think all ordinary Vikings had mail coats like the one shown on page 32?

Swords, spear, arrow and axeheads, helmet and shield used by Vikings.

Here are two Viking warriors from the sagas.

Gunnar was tall and strong and well skilled in the use of arms. He could wield the sword and deal blows so swiftly that three swords seemed to flash through the air at the same time. He had no equal in shooting with a bow. In full armour he could leap higher than his own height and jump as far backwards as forwards.

Njal's Saga

Thorolf had a broad solid shield and a very strong helmet on his head and a sword by his side he called 'Long'. In his hand he had a spear with a broad blade and thick shaft.

Egil's Saga

1. What weapons did these two Vikings use?
2. Why was Gunnar such a remarkable fighter?
3. Do you think Thorolf's spear was for throwing or for jabbing?
4. Draw a picture of the Viking shield Kari carried in the opening story. Remember to colour and decorate it.

Battle Tactics

During the adventures described in *Grettir's Saga*, the hero arrives to stay with a family that is being terrorised by a gang led by a man called Snaekoll. Snaekoll was a special kind of Viking fighter called a 'berserk' and Grettir offers to fight him.

The berserk was sitting on his horse wearing his helmet and he had before him a shield bound with iron and looked terribly threatening. He began to howl and bite the rim of his shield. He held the shield up to his mouth and scowled over the upper edge like a madman. Grettir kicked the shield with such force it struck the berserk's mouth and broke his jaw. He dragged him off his horse and cut off his head. Snaekoll's followers fled.

Grettir's Saga

1. Why was a berserk such a terrifying Viking warrior?
2. Why do you think he behaved so terrifyingly?

Many Vikings thought Odin's powers helped berserks. Most Viking battles consisted of individuals fighting one another in a great, noisy, terrifying confusion. At the front raged berserks like these described in a poem written in Viking times:

> Cried then the bear pelted,
> Courage they had thoughts of,
> Wailed then the wolf coated,
> And weapons brandished.
>
> *Haraldskaei*

1. Try and write this poem in your own words.

Large armies of Vikings did sometimes have a proper battle formation. The most popular was a wedge shape, pointing at the enemy and led by a chief with whom stood a standard bearer. One such leader, Ragnar, had a white

One of the Lewis chessmen, probably meant to represent a berserk.

standard decorated with a picture of Odin's ravens. Ragnar is supposed to have earned the nickname 'Hairy Breeches' by wearing animal skins, hair side out and smeared in pitch and sand. In these he was able to face the fiery breath of a dragon and even poisonous snakes.

1. Look back at Chapter 5. In what ways did their ships help Vikings to catch their enemies by surprise?

Vikings also built strong defences. In the south of Denmark they created a long and massive wall, the Danework. In Denmark places like this have also been found:

1. What do you think this used to be in Viking times?
2. What do you think the buildings once contained?
3. In the gaps in the outer walls what would there have once been to make attack from outside more difficult?

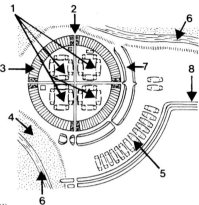

Plan of Trelleborg Fort and an aerial view of Trelleborg Fort today.

1 16 barracks buildings arranged in squares
2 gateway (4 in all)
3 bank of turf and timber 7 metres high
4 marshy land
5 houses (possibly built later, the fort site being full)
6 river
7 ditch
8 outer defences of earth wall and ditch

35

The Viking Fury hits Europe

(This would be a good time to tackle Workguide 6, No. 1.)

Places raided by Vikings in Europe

795	Lindisfarne, Northumbria
834	Beginning of a series of raids on French coast
839	Turgeis leads Viking attack on Northumbria. From 835, many raids on England.
841	Danes attack northern France, burn Rouen and other places along River Seine.
843	Vikings raid up the River Loire and burn Nantes
844	Vikings sail up River Garonne and attack Toulouse then raid northern Spain – but are beaten away by local people.
845	Ragnar leads Vikings on raids up the River Seine, beats a French Army near Paris.
846	Vikings raid northern Germany, sail up River Elbe
859	Swedish Vikings capture Novgorod in northern Russia.
859	Vikings led by Bjorn Ironside and Hastings sail from River Seine and raid round Europe's coast as far as north-west Italy.
860	Rurik leads Swedish Vikings to conquer Russia's Baltic coast. Askold and Dir lead a Viking raid across Russia to attack Constantinople.
879	Oleg succeeds Rurik. Captures Kiev.
885–6	Vikings beseige Paris.
889	New Viking attack on Paris beaten off.
907 & 912	Fresh Viking raids on Constantinople.
911–12	Rollo establishes a Viking dukedom in Normandy.

1. How far from their homelands did Vikings travel to raid other lands?
2. In what centuries did Viking raids take place?
3. Can you think of reasons why Vikings raided and conquered other lands?

At the time, Adam of Bremen thought

Vikings wander the world because poverty drives them from their homelands and they bring home as booty what other countries produce in plenty.

Some historians think some Vikings searched overseas for food – and even homes – because their lands were becoming too crowded. By 800 they had ships that could travel long distances and many Vikings seem to have set off for adventures.
    One saga writer has described how Viking raids began.

In the summer they went on Viking voyages, conquered land and divided the spoils among themselves. In the winter they stayed at home.
Egil's Saga

But gradually Vikings began sailing off in larger numbers, staying through the winter in strong bases in foreign lands, and even settling there for good with their families. People watching Vikings come to their lands have left accounts full of gloom and despair. This is the scene described by a writer in France.

The dead lay everywhere. Priests and laymen, women and children and infants. The Franks were filled with despair. The Christian lands seemed doomed to destruction.

Annals of St Bertun

The accounts we have of what it was like to be attacked by Vikings were usually written by monks and priests for few other people could write. The Vikings were not Christians and saw no reason why they shouldn't attack religious buildings which often had treasures in them. Only unarmed clergy stood in their way. People already living in Christian lands quite often fought one another, but probably did not as a rule attack holy places.

The sudden and unexpected appearance of Viking forces must have made them seem especially alarming, and there is no doubt that they were very brave fighters.

1. What reasons have been suggested to explain why Vikings went on raids overseas?
2. Why do you think Vikings attacked churches and monasteries so often?

Some Viking Raids

Europe was not really peaceful before the Vikings came. Kings and princes quarrelled and sometimes fought each other. But most of Germany and France were well organized under one ruler, Charles the Great.

Some years after Charles the Great died the empire was split between three brothers. A monk of the time, called Ermentarius of Noirmoutier, wrote

Because the brothers fought each other, enemies from outside grew stronger. Coasts were left unguarded and more and more ships kept coming bringing Norsemen.

1. Explain in your own words why Europe became an easy target for the Vikings.

In 843 a fleet of 67 Viking ships sailed up the River Loire, captured the town of Nantes, then stayed the winter nearby. It was the first powerful Viking raid deep into France. The Vikings not only sailed up rivers, they anchored their boats, captured horses and galloped across the countryside to attack places where wealth was to be found.

In 885 Paris was attacked by a force supposed to number 700 ships. Its leader, Sigfrid, found Paris ready to fight and for a year he tried in all sorts of ways to capture it.

1. In what ways, can you suggest, might the Vikings have tried to break into a city?

The Vikings made three huge siege engines out of an enormous oak. Thousands of lead balls from slings fell like hail on the city and powerful catapults were fired at the walls. They raised their painted shields above their heads and charged. Three times they tried to fill the moat and break the walls with battering rams. The defenders poured flaming oil on the siege engines and set them on fire.

Abbo of Fleury

Paris held out, the King arrived and paid the Vikings to go away.

But part of France was so much under Viking control that King Charles decided to let them stay. He made Rollo, the Viking leader there, Duke of Normandy. Rollo became a Christian and agreed to accept Charles as his King. But according to a popular legend he would not carry out the ceremony of kissing the King's foot. He ordered one of his men to do it instead.

The Northman bent down and seized the King's foot and stood up to kiss it, throwing the King on his back amid roars of laughter.

William of Jumierges

1. What do you think this event tells us about the Vikings?

Another remarkable Viking force, led by Hastings and Bjorn Ironside went on a campaign that lasted three years. On their wanderings they fought in France, clashed with the Moors of Spain, Algeria and Morocco. At Luna in Italy they faced a strongly defended town.

How they captured Luna was written down 150 years later by Dean Dudo. Hastings pretended to be dying and persuaded the townspeople he wanted to become a Christian and be buried in Luna. He is supposed to have said to his men

'Tell their Bishop and Duke I have died. Beg them in tears to let me be buried in their town. Lay me out like a corpse, but with my weapons by me and you surround me as mourners.' The foolish townsfolk let in the sad procession. Hastings leapt up, his men threw off their cloaks and they killed those about them. They held open the town gates, the rest of the Vikings rushed in and captured Luna.

Roger of Wendover, *Flowers of History* (adapted)

In the Byzantine Empire Viking forces tried to capture the great city of Constantinople. They found they had to face a new weapon.

1. Look at the picture on the left. What are the men using? Is it like any modern weapon?
2. Why would it do great damage to Viking ships?

Vikings in the area eventually changed sides and joined the Emperor of Byzantium to fight in his Varangian Guard.

The people in the left-hand boat are working Greek fire.

7 The Vikings in Britain

The First Raids

Three strange ships approached the coast of south-west England. It was the year 789. The royal official for the area, Beaduheard, hurried to the shore to meet the men. He expected them to be traders and asked them to come to the royal palace. But the strangers killed Beaduheard.

This is the first Viking raid on Britain that we know about. It was soon followed by another.

In the year 793 terrible signs appeared in the sky over Northumbria and frightened the people. There were whirlwinds and flashes of lightening and fiery dragons seemed to be flying in the air. A great famine followed and a little after a heathen attack destroyed God's church on Lindisfarne with plunder and slaughter.

Both these stories come from *The Anglo-Saxon Chronicle* which was started in the late ninth century and continued in following years. Lindisfarne monks may well have carved the stone illustrated on this page.

1. Which of these two raids do you think was the more serious?
2. Do you think the 'terrible signs' were really warnings of Viking attack?

Carving from a tombstone at Lindisfarne.

This treasure from St. Ninian's Isle, Shetland, is an example of the kind of treasure the Vikings hoped to seize on raids.

3. What sort of weapons are the Viking raiders holding?

The twelfth-century Englishman, Simeon of Durham, thought the Viking raiders were

like stinging hornets, spreading on all sides like fearful wolves. They robbed and slaughtered not only sheep and oxen, but even priests and monks and nuns.

Simeon of Durham, *History of the Kings*

1. Do these sound like the Vikings you read about in the early chapters of this book?

For another 250 years Viking raiders kept coming to Britain.

1. Would you go on risky raids for treasure like this? Why?
2. What other reasons might Vikings have for coming to Britain?

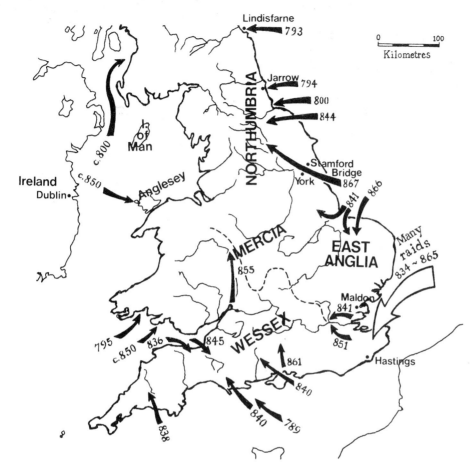

Places in England and Wales raided by the Vikings.

Vikings in Scotland

1. Look at the map of Europe in Workguide 6. Why were Norwegian Vikings likely to come to Scotland?

One of the sagas says that a Viking called Ketil Flatnose

> preferred to go west across the sea to Scotland because the living was good there. He knew the country well for he had raided there extensively.
>
> *Laxdaela Saga*

King Harold Fairhair sailed west to punish Vikings who raided the coasts of Norway all summer and wintered in Orkney and Shetland. He defeated them and went to the Isle of Man and the Hebrides. Harold then gave Sigurd the title of 'Earl'.

Orkneyinga Saga

Sigurd became the first of the Viking Earls of the Northern Isles.

1. Look carefully at this map. The country is divided into several kingdoms. Write down the names of these kingdoms.
2. Why would it help the Vikings to attack a country split into several kingdoms?
3. Look where Vikings raided. Why do you think they attacked river areas so often?

1. Why do you think Norwegian raiders like Ketil were themselves attacked by the King of Norway? (In fact Ketil left Scotland for Iceland to escape King Harald.)
2. Does the island in the photograph (foot of page 41) look like a good place for a Viking base?

It was here at Birsay, an islet off Orkney, that a capital for the earl was built by the greatest of them, Thorfinn the Mighty. Vikings settled down to farm and fish in dwellings scattered among the isles. Archaeologists looking for remains of their homes were helped, in 1897, by a great storm which shifted sands at Jarlshof on the southern tip of Shetland. This is what appeared:

1. *What is the building made of?*
2. *Does it remind you of any house seen in Chapter 2?*
3. *Why do you think it is not made of timber?*

Jarlshof, Shetland.

Aerial view of Birsay in the Orkneys.

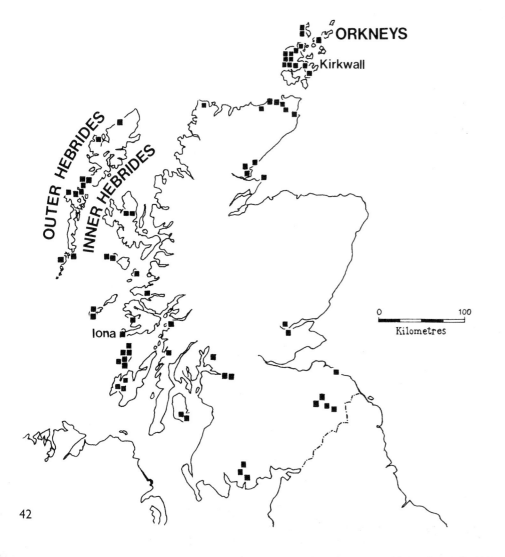

The location of Viking finds in Scotland.

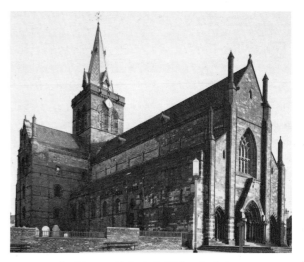

St. Magnus Cathedral, Kirkwall, Orkney.

The building above was also made for Vikings.

1. What sort of a building is it?
2. What does it tell you about the way Viking beliefs changed?

Look at the map on this page.

1. Do the Vikings seem to have settled in Scotland in large numbers?
2. Can you think why most Vikings came to Western Scotland?

Viking control of the isles made them a nuisance sometimes to Scottish kings, but they weren't the danger they were to prove to be in England.

1. Trace the map of Scotland and colour in the places where Vikings settled. Write in the names of Birsay, Jarlshof and Kirkwall.

The Danelaw is created

Most Vikings who came to England were Danes. In 850 a force stayed the winter on the island of Thanet in the Thames, instead of returning home.

1. Why do you think they felt able to risk staying?

In 865 a very large Danish army arrived, led by three brothers. The brothers were called Ivar the Boneless, Ubbi and Halfdan. According to Viking saga legends, they had come for revenge. Their father, Ragnar, was supposed to have been killed by King Ella of Northumbria who had thrown him into a pit of poisonous snakes. The army was too strong for most English kings. King Ella was killed, much of the north and middle of the country was conquered. But in Wessex the Great Army was halted at the Battle of Ashdown by Saxons led by King Ethelred and his brother Alfred. The Great Army divided and while one section stayed in the south, Halfdan led the rest north. According to *The Anglo-Saxon Chronicle*

In 876 Halfdan shared out the land of the Northumbrians. They proceeded to plough and support themselves.

1. How can you tell from the map on p.40 and the list of place name endings where many Vikings settled to live?

2. Look at an atlas map of Britain and see if you can find some more examples of Viking place names.

Common Viking place-name endings

thwaite – field	both – temporary shelter (eg Boothby)
thorpe – village	wide – creek or inlet
beck – river, stream	ey and a (as endings, eg Orkney, Ronaldsha)
by – farm or bigger settlement, even town	ford – used to mean a water passage (eg Milford), where it means 'river crossing' it is English.
toft – homestead	
gill – ravine	
fell – hill	
force – waterfall	
tarn – pond	

1. What kind of work was probably carried out by Vikings living in the place illustrated below?
2. Since this is an isolated Viking farm, what does it tell you about how Vikings in the Danelaw were regarded by the English?

Excavation at Ribblehead Farm, Yorkshire.

Excavations at York.

Fragments of wooden bowls, carved antler work and stone carving found at York.

Some Vikings settled in towns, especially in the city of Jorvik (or York).

Here you can see the heart of Viking York being uncovered by archaeologists. The Vikings lived in timber houses.

1. What kind of Viking craftsmen must have lived in York to make objects like those illustrated on this page and opposite?

An English monk of Viking times wrote

York is made richer by the treasure of merchants who came from all quarters, especially the Danish people.

Life of St Oswald

It would be quite wrong to think the Vikings brought nothing but ruin to Britain. They were good farmers, clever craftsmen and hardworking traders. They did not kill off the English of the Danelaw but mixed with them and became Christians. William of Malmesbury, who lived in the early twelfth century, thought that by the tenth century:

The Northumbrians were already mingled with the Danes in one race.

1. Can you think of any reasons why the Vikings settled in England in greater numbers than in Scotland?
2. How do we know what part of the country was within the Danelaw?

The Success of the Kingdom of Wessex

These are entries from *The Anglo-Saxon Chronicle*

878. The enemy army drove a great many of the English people across the sea and conquered most of the others and the people gave in to them except King Alfred. He travelled in difficulties through the woods and fens with a small force. He made a stronghold at Athelney. Then, at Edington, he fought against the whole army and put it to flight and pursued it. The enemy swore they would leave his kingdom.
893. The King divided his army in two so that always half the men were at home, half on service, apart from men who guarded the burghs.
896. Alfred had long ships built to oppose the Danish warships. They were almost twice as long as the Danes', some had sixty oars and some more. They were swifter and steadier and also higher than the enemy's.

1. Why was Alfred able to dodge his enemies?
2. How did Alfred improve his army?
3. Why do you think he had to let so many of his men go home? Is this how armies today are organized?
4. How did Alfred try and beat the Danes before they could land?

(You can read more about Alfred, if you wish, in *Alfred and the Danes*, a *Then and There* book.)

Ethelred and Canute

In 978 a twelve-year-old boy, Ethelred, became King of England. Viking forces, realising England was not well led, soon returned to the attack. Even when grown up Ethelred was not a good leader, and he earned a name that nowadays is written as 'the Unready' though really it means 'lacking in wise advice'. Some local Saxon leaders tried to stop the Vikings. In 991 Bryhtnoth led such a force and fought the battle of Maldon which a Saxon poet made the subject of a poem. Viking raiders approached the Essex coast and sent a messenger to speak to the defenders.

Then stood on strand and called out sternly
A Viking spokesman. He made a speech,
'The swift striking seafarers send me to thee.
Bid me say that thou send for thy safety
rings, bracelets. Better for you
that you stay straightway our onslaught with tribute
than that we should share bitter strife.'
The Battle of Maldon

Bryhtnoth would not bribe the Vikings and died, vainly trying to stop them.
In *St Olaf's Saga* another Viking force, led by Olaf the Stout, tied ropes to London Bridge and pulled it down because it blocked the way up the Thames. *The Anglo-Saxon Chronicle* records that drunken Vikings even killed the Archbishop of Canterbury:

Leather knife sheath found in York excavations.

Here are two more entries from *The Anglo-Saxon Chronicle*

1010. When the enemy was in the east, then our forces gathered in the west. When they were in the south our forces were in the north. In the end there was no leader willing to raise forces but each fled as quickly as he could.

Danes went about burning and slaying, and the English forces caused the people every sort of harm too.

1. What do these accounts tell you about the sort of leader Ethelred was?
2. When Ethelred was finally defeated, why do you think many English people would be relieved?

England's new king was the Viking, Canute. A saga writer said of him

he was a man of great good luck in everything to do with power.

Knytlinga Saga

For 20 years he brought England peace. He made his Viking followers obey the laws. He married Ethelred's widow, Emma. He was a Christian who went on a pilgrimage to Rome.

1. What did Canute do that made the English ready to accept him as their ruler?
2. Look at the map. What problems might Canute have faced in ruling all these countries?

Canute's Empire.
(Norway was part of his empire for 6 or 7 years only.)

They pelted him with bones and oxheads, and one of them struck him a blow on the head with the back of his axe so that he sank down and died.

The last Viking Attack on England

Canute died in 1035 and England was soon under the rule of a Saxon, Edward the Confessor. When Edward died in 1066 one of the last great Vikings, Harald Hardrada, King of Norway, decided to try and conquer England. He started off with 200 ships, and picked up help from the Scottish isles and English rebels till he had a mighty force of 300 ships. On September 20th, the Vikings sailed up river into Yorkshire, landed, and easily beat local resistance. But as they were settling down to plan more conquests they themselves were taken by surprise. A large English force appeared, as if from nowhere, and at Stamford Bridge the Vikings were beaten and Harald Hardrada killed.

The man who won this battle was Harold Godwinsson. He had been chosen by the English to rule over them, and had shown he was a fine leader by the energy with which he had rushed his men two hundred miles north to beat the Vikings. Yet, nineteen days after his victory, King Harold lay dead. From France another enemy had crossed to England.

The picture below shows some of the Norman soldiers who ended Harold's short reign. Their leader, William, was a descendant of the Viking chief, Rollo, who became Duke of Normandy. But the Norman victory meant that England was now linked to France, not Scandinavia. The great Viking days were over. Europe was now well organized to fight the Viking threat. The Vikings themselves were organized by their kings and no longer able to raid as they pleased. The great adventurers who had troubled Europe for two and a half centuries settled down to become just another group of Europeans.

Scene from the Bayeux Tapestry showing the Normans who attacked the Saxons at the battle of Hastings. Note the single Saxon soldier (a housecarle) on foot in the extreme right-hand side of the picture.

Bibliography

School books
K. Allen, *The Vikings*, Purnell, 1973.
D. R. Barker, *The Vikings at Home and Abroad*, Arnold, 1966.
L. Dickinson Rich, *The First Book of the Vikings*, Franklin Watts, 1962.
F. R. Donovan, *The Vikings*, Cassell (*Caravel*), 1964.
S. C. George, *The Vikings*, David & Charles, 1973.
M. Gibson, *The Vikings*, Wayland Press, 1972.
B. Henry, *Vikings and Norsemen*, John Baker, 1971.
G. Middleton, *Saxons and Vikings*, Longman (*Focus on History*), 1968.
A. Murton Carter, *One Day with the Vikings*, Tyndall, 1973.
M. Neurath & J. Ellis, *They Lived Like This: The Vikings*, Macdonald, 1970.
G. Onclinex, *Einar the Viking*, A & C Black, 1969.
J. Platt, *The Vikings*, Macmillan (*Active History*), 1972.
G. L. Proctor, *The Vikings*, Longman (*Then and There*), 1959.
J. Simpson, *Everyday Life in the Viking Age*, Batsford, 1967.

General histories
J. Brondsted, *The Vikings*, Penguin, 1960.
P. G. Foote & D. M. Wilson, *The Viking Achievement*, Sidgewick & Jackson, 1970.
R. A. Hall, *The Viking Kingdom of York*, Yorkshire Museum, 1976.
G. Jones, *A History of the Vikings*, Oxford, 1968.
M. Magnusson, *The Viking Expansion Westwards*, Bodley Head, 1973.
M. Magnusson, *Vikings, Saints or Sinners?* Yorkshire Philosophical Society, 1975.
E. Oxenstierna, *The Norsemen*, Studio Vista, 1966.
R. Poertner, *The Vikings*, St James Press, 1975.
P. H. Sawyer, *The Age of the Vikings*, Arnold, 1971.
D. Wilson, *The Vikings and Their Origins*, Thames & Hudson, 1970.

Sagas and Chronicles
Adam of Bremen, *History of the Archbishops of Hamburg-Bremen* (Trans. F. J. Tschan), Columbia University, 1959.
The Anglo-Saxon Chronicle (Trans. G. N. Garmonsway), Dent, 1953.
Egil's Saga (Trans. C. Fell), Dent, 1975.
C. Gibson, *The Two Olafs of Norway*, Dobson, 1968.
R. L. Green, *The Myths of the Norsemen*, Penguin, 1960.
G. Jones, *Scandinavian Legends and Folk Tales*, Oxford, 1956.
Snorri Sturluson, *A History of the Kings of Norway* (Trans. L. M. Hollander), University of Texas, 1964.
The Vinland Sagas (Trans. M. Magnusson & H. Palsson), Penguin, 1965.
D. Whitelock (ed.), *English Historical Documents*, Vol. I, Eyre & Spottiswoode, 1955.